TOO MUCH HOLLY, NOT ENOUGH HOLY?

Too Much Holly, Not Enough Holy?

Searching for Christmas

Patricia Wilson

THE UPPER ROOM
Nashville, Tennessee

TOO MUCH HOLLY, NOT ENOUGH HOLY?

Scripture quotations are from the King James Version of the Bible.

Book and Cover Design: Nancy G. Johnstone
Cover Transparency: Stephen Tonks
First Printing: September 1987 (7)
Library of Congress Catalog Card Number: 87-050702
ISBN: 0-8358-0566-2

Printed in the United States of America

For Christine,

of course.

CONTENTS

PREFACE

Come and sit with me as I write letters to my friend, Christine. We knew each other in the big city of Toronto, but now I live in rural Ontario and Christine lives on the other side of this continent, in a manse with her minister husband and teenage daughter. We have been friends for many years. Because distance now separates us, we often write to each other of the frustrations and joys of our respective lives.

I write to Chris of my search for a "real" Christmas, but much of what I write is of a search that is common to us all. And Chris's responses, both real and perceived, are the same as you might feel.

While you read these letters, be for a time my friend Chris. I am writing to you of the desire of Christians everywhere to truly celebrate the birthday of our King. But more importantly, I'm writing of the reality of Christmas today—the rush, the bother, the worry, the anxiety—and of my determination somehow to stop playing the Christmas game of today's world.

Can I do it? Can I opt out entirely? Can I find peace in the madness of the season? Like a good mystery story, only the final chapter gives the answers. Or, to put it in a Christmas metaphor, the final proof is in the pudding.

1.

TOO MUCH HOLLY, NOT ENOUGH HOLY?

Peace I leave with you, my peace I give unto you: not as the world giveth, give I unto you. —John 14:27

January 6

Dear Christine,

This morning I woke up with the same feeling I get after my annual visit to the dentist: Thank goodness that's over for another year! Christmas has come and finally gone, and I am glad to see the last of it.

I have just savored the pleasures of a tree-free living room, a card-free mantelpiece, and a turkey-free refrigerator. I have watered the poinsettia, thrown out the empty chocolate boxes, and now I am going to enjoy the postseason silence and catch up on my letter-writing.

We had a hectic Christmas, as usual. Lots of parties, lots of cooking, lots of shopping, and lots of headaches. You know that feeling you get after riding a merry-go-round? Well, I feel as if I stepped on a merry-go-round sometime last October, and have only just stepped off. I'm still dizzy.

I can't think where the last three months have gone. It seems like only last week that I was buying wool to knit Christmas sweaters for everyone. I got some of that super-bulky stuff that you knit on telephone-pole-sized needles. Quick Knits, they call them. It seemed like a possible undertaking at the time. Ah well, I still have the wool, and one back and two arms are done. Maybe if I start within the next hour, they'll be ready for next Christmas.

Do you know, Chris, I actually met a lady who does start her Christmas knitting in January? Now, that's planning ahead! Do you suppose she breezes through December smiling serenely, totally above the shopping-crazed crowds in every store? Just think, she'd be missing out on the thrill of the chase: the search for the perfect gift, in size 8 petite, in green, without buttons, trimmed in black, washable, and under ten dollars. I'd hate to miss that, wouldn't you?

I've put on eight pounds since I last wrote to you. I figured it out. That's an average of two pounds, ten ounces a week. Or, nearly six ounces a day. Or, to get down to the raw truth, I'm talking the equivalent of ten chocolates or five slices of turkey (dark meat) or two pieces of fruitcake or a large handful of salted nuts each and every day over the past three weeks. You'd think that if I now stopped eating chocolates, turkey, fruit-cake, and salted nuts, those eight pounds would simply melt away, but you and I know that they'll linger until the bathing-suit season, and I'll spend most of May eating lettuce and water. I guess you could call that my penance for Christmas indulgences. Just once, I'd like to wake up on January 1 and weigh exactly the same as I did on December 1.

I have decided that I am not going to reply to all those people who sent me their annual "form" letter. Some Christmas mail is almost as bad as getting mail addressed to "Occupant." I can see you smiling, Chris. "Sour grapes," you're saying. All right, I confess. I didn't get time to send out our annual letter this year. I think it got lost somewhere between October and December.

Have you noticed that Christmas cards are coming back in style? For awhile, we received a dozen at the most, but this year I ran out of space by mid-December and had to resort to those colored clotheslines with the matching poinsettia pins. I strung them all across the family room, and I must admit, it looks a little bare in there today. I'd gotten used to the beaming santas, puppy dogs in stockings, and dancing candy canes. However, to be perfectly honest with you, Christine, I wish people hadn't put us back on their list. Now, I'm really going to have to get organized if I'm going to get that many cards out in return. When you only have a half a dozen to send, you can wait to the last minute and send them airmail. (Remember the year I sent your card by courier?) But we can't afford to do that with a large number. Maybe I should break down and buy one of those Christmas card diary things that lists everyone's name and address and the dates that they sent you cards. You check off when you send cards in return, and that way, no one gets missed. Considering that I have yet to keep any kind of diary up to date, perhaps I should consider a pre-Christmas card instead—say in August!

Actually, that's not a good idea, either. August is already a busy Christmas month. That's when I work on my allotment of crafts for the church bazaar. By the way, thanks for sending me that pattern for the toilet roll cover. It was a real winner, although I have to confess, Gerald will never shower in a room that has a hot-pink poodle in attendance. Can you send me the pattern for the matching toothbrush holder this year? I think I'm on a roll, and it sure beats trying to find something new, different, cute, and cheap to make for the bazaar table. Did you ever stop to work out how much these crafts actually cost? I mean, if you added up the time spent shopping for the materials, the hours of actual labor, the packaging and pricing, not to mention time at the actual bazaar, one hot-pink poodle toilet roll cover would probably sell for seventy-five dollars! Occasionally, I'm tempted to just donate the cash, but that would take all the fun out of it, wouldn't it? Wouldn't it? And anyway, what would I do with all that free time when I wasn't crocheting poodles?

Do you detect a slight note of bitterness here? Perhaps it's just postseason depression speaking. Perhaps it's the result of an overdose of "Jingle Bells" and Santa Claus. Or maybe it's just too much holly and not enough holy.

What happened to Christmas, Christine? Where did the baby Jesus go? Was he shoved out of the manger by a red-nosed reindeer? Has an overweight man in a red suit taken over the season? Did the birthday celebration lose out to the annual office bash?

How come I'm glad it's all over? Christmas should be the highlight of my Christian year. It should be a time when I can come to the manger and find peace in my life. Instead, I spend the entire season in a frenzy of doing, doing, doing.

Some celebration! Some peace!

Later: OK. I've thought it over, and I'm going to make a New Year's resolution right now. This year, Christmas is going to be different. Christmas is going to be Christ-centered. It's going to be Christian. It's going to be a celebration of a holy birth.

As of now, I resolve not to get caught up in this world's Christmas. You're my witness, Chris.

I'll keep you posted. Thanks for being my friendly shoulder to whine on.

Love and a hug to all,

Pat

2.

BARGAINS IN CONVENTION CITY!

Lord, thou hast heard the desire of the humble: thou wilt prepare their heart, thou wilt cause thine ear to hear.
—Psalm 10:17

March 24

Dear Christine,

Here I am in Convention City. It is not as sunny as the picture on this hotel stationery might lead you to believe. Some of the ladies told me about some fantastic bargains in a special Christmas store here. Imagine buying Christmas wrapping paper and ribbon in March. No, I have not forgotten my resolution. I am simply thinking ahead to avoid the usual last-minute rush that spoils the season. This year, I'm going to be ready to savor every moment of the birthday celebration.

Kiss and a hug to all,

Pat

PS. My mother always wrapped all her Christmas presents in brown-paper grocery bags, or in the bags from the stores where she bought them. I'm beginning to wonder whether she had the right idea. As she said, "Who notices the wrapping paper? It's what's inside that's important." Actually, Chris, I remember being excited when the Neiman-Marcus bag had my name on it. Mother's wrapping paper has always been a family joke, but I'm sure she never spent hours cutting, wrapping, tying, pasting, and sticking.

Do you think my family is ready for brown-paper bags? Do you think I am?

PPS. These year-round Christmas stores are becoming really popular. I wonder if we could call the church a year-round Christmas store for Christians? What would that say about shopping early?

Pat

3.

DEAR OCCUPANT: MERRY CHRISTMAS

Ye are our epistle written on our hearts, known and read of all men —2 Corinthians 3:2

May 21

Dear Christine,

Guess what? I've signed up for a calligraphy course. I've always wanted to learn how to do all that beautiful writing, and now I'm going to. One evening a week for four weeks; they've promised me I'll be an expert.

I have to confess, though, that there is an ulterior motive to my enthusiasm. Remember when I wrote to you and said that we had received an awful lot of Christmas cards last year, and that we would have to reciprocate this year? Well, I've been giving the whole thing some thought. If I'm going to get back into the Christmas card business, then I'd like to do it with some style. I'd like to send out the kind of Christmas cards that people keep in their bottom kitchen drawer because they're too pretty to throw out. Eventually, they'll go to school with the kids for a craft day, and some teacher will keep them for her kitchen drawer because they're too pretty to cut up. You know the kind of card I'm talking about.

The problem is that kind of card costs a fortune to buy. That is, if you can find one.

Whatever happened to the Christmas cards we used to get? You know, the ones with the verses that rhymed and the hand-colored snow scenes with sparkle glued

on; or the ones that unfolded into a stand-up manger
scene for the top of the television. Remember the cards
that had a kind of velvet texture on Mary's dress? I can
still feel the fuzzy surface under my fingers. Or remember the gold gilt on the Wise Men's crowns that looked
real? I always liked the cards with the iridescent rain-
bows that changed color when you wiggled them.

I wonder who decided that "pretty" had to go. Was it
the same person who thought that modern quips were
better than sentimental rhymes? Did he (she?) also
decide that Christmas was best represented by a lot of
inanimate objects, and that anything "religious" would
never sell? Last year, I counted seventeen reindeer;
twelve mice; three snowmen; and innumerable kittens,
puppies, and elves all doing silly things, like toboggan-
ing or skating or popping out of stockings. Not to mention that fat man in the red suit lurking in chimneys.
Most of the cards wished that Santa would be "good" to
me. The tacky prize went to the card with the inebriated
reindeer on the front and the words "Bingle Jells" inside. (The senders are not going on my list.) On the
"religious" side, there were seven sets of praying
hands. No doubt there is some social significance in
that fact, but I'm darned if I'm going to look for it.

Hence my calligraphy course. I am going to make my
own cards this year. Something simple, something
meaningful, something that will express the true meaning of Christmas. No, I don't know just what, but I'm
sure something will come to mind. At the moment, I'm
concentrating on learning how to make a capital P that
doesn't look like a capital A.

How did we ever get into this Christmas card business, anyway? I can understand that they're a good way to keep in touch with people who live far away, but I get cards from people at work. These are people whom I see every day, talk to regularly, yet they send me a Christmas card. Wouldn't it be easier just to stop me in the hall, wish me Merry Christmas, and leave it at that? I receive cards from companies, for heaven's sakes! Can I really believe that the local supermarket wants me to have a season of joy? Or that my bank manager (whom I have never met and have only spoken to once on the phone) is wishing the best for my family? Or that Joe's Garage values my patronage and hopes I'll have a safe and happy New Year? Something has gone terribly wrong here. Christmas cards have become a corporate business obligation.

OK, Chris, I'm going to forget the calligraphy! I'll just send out my business card next year. To show that I'm in the Christmas spirit, I'll stick a pretty seal on each one: candles, reindeer, poinsettias, praying hands, bells, holly, angels, whatever my mood dictates. How's that for innovative, creative thinking?

I almost got caught, didn't I, Chris? I almost jumped into the Christmas card trap. I would have been frantically calligraphing cards right up to Christmas Eve. Most of them would have been for people I hardly know: people who sent me cards last year, for whatever reason, and to whom I now feel obligated, for whatever reason. Well, I'm not going to play!

I'm sending cards to my friends, to people I love and care about, people I can't physically hug and wish Merry Christmas. I'll send you one. But if you lived next door, I'd invite you over for coffee instead.

I think I will send out hand-drawn cards after all. That is, if I pass my calligraphy course, and if I can come up with a simple design that expresses the true meaning of Christmas and takes under thirty seconds to execute.

Any ideas? Me neither.

Love and a hug,

Pat

4.

MARTYRDOM ON THE BEACH

Let all your things be done with charity.
                              —1 Corinthians 16:14

July 14

Dear Christine,

Happy Birthday! Thought I'd send you a quick note and greetings from the sunny skies of cottage country. Have started my sweaters for Christmas. Hate knitting in the summer. Hate knitting on the beach—hot, sticky, sandy, and damp. Hate knitting, period! But, I'm going to finish these darn things, no matter what. You can bet that I'm letting everyone within a hundred yards know how wonderful I am to be knitting in this heat. One finished, two to go!

Poor me sends you all a hug.

Saint Pat of the Needles!

Next Day: The Knitting Martyr has been burned at the stake. Sunburned, that is. I'm now redder and wiser. I remembered that part of my New Year's resolution was to savor the real Christmas season. Knitting on the beach in July in a fit of "poor me" is not "real" Christmas. When and if I can knit those sweaters just because I really want to (rather than because I have to), then I'll start again. Onward to freedom.

Pat

PS. The "want to" will come from the love I want to express for my family. All gifts should be on that basis. (I suspect that the baby Jesus came to us from a "want to" motive, not from a "have to" one!)

5.

SEND 'EM A CHECK

Which of you, intending to build a tower, sitteth not down first, and counteth the cost, whether he have sufficient to finish it? —Luke 14:28

August 29

Dear Christine,

The first cold tendrils of reality have brushed against my New Year's resolution. We had the bazaar worknight last night, and I had a game plan all ready. I was going to offer them a fat check and then check out.

All I could think about was the time that would now be available to me, time that had previously been spent crocheting pink poodles and making plastic Dixie cup bells. I would have whole hours in which to contemplate the true meaning of Christmas. I envisioned myself in meaningful meditation, undisturbed by the guilt of unfinished pinecone wreaths. Opting out of the bazaar would be my first strike for a Christian Christmas.

I never even got to first base. The check is still in my purse, right beside the pattern for a tree ornament made from margarine tub tops. (Enclosed with this letter—I thought you might like it for your bazaar.)

As you know, Chris, I am not an avid meeting attender. In fact, on a list of things I'd like to do, I'd rate cleaning the bathtub or grooming the dog before going to a meeting. So, it was with some reluctance that I agreed to go to the worknight. Actually, the reason I went stems from when I was a teenager. I was always the one who wouldn't break up with a boyfriend over the phone, thinking it more humane to do it face-to-face, and I suppose it was a similar kind of thinking that made me attend the meeting. Just sending in a check would have been easier but more cowardly.

Chris, have you ever had the feeling that somebody up there has set you up? You know, that feeling that everything that happens is divinely planned to speak to you. Do you occasionally hear the angels chuckling at your expense? That's how it was at the worknight.

Even though the meeting was meant to be a working session, we still had to attend to the formalities: roll call, scripture reading, meditation, prayer, and hymn. Mrs. Baine, our president, called the meeting to order and asked us to name our favorite Christmas carol, "just to put us in the right mood for the evening." She asked me to start.

Well, I was ready to let them have it. I'd not only give them a carol title, but also a small speech on my new attitude toward Christmas. It didn't quite work out the way I had planned.

Occasionally, much to my embarrassment, I forget words, names of people, and things. Once I even forgot Gerald's name when I was introducing him to some friends. Well, it happened again. Only this time, I forgot the name of a Christmas carol. You're not going to believe this, Christine, but the only title I could think of was "Jingle Bells." I suppose it could have been worse. I suppose "Rudolph, the Red-Nosed Reindeer" or "Santa Claus Is Coming to Town" might have caused a bigger stir, but I doubt it. I made some inane remark about being a part of today's Christmas world, but I don't think they bought it. Somehow, the moment wasn't right to make my "freedom" speech.

Mrs. Clark gave a brief meditation. Now, usually I can count on Mrs. Clark to read something light, often a rhyming verse with a cute twist of phrase at the end. But this evening she dove into Oswald Chambers' book *My Utmost for His Highest*. The topic was "The Worship of the Work," and one line really struck home. It was, "There is no responsibility on you for the work; the only responsibility you have is to keep in living, constant touch with God, and to see that you allow nothing to hinder your cooperation with Him." Ouch! About this time, I began to wish that I'd just broken up over the phone; that is, sent the check and stayed home.

It got worse. Mrs. Bellows handed out our memory verse for the evening, Ecclesiastes 9:10: "Whatsoever thy hand findeth to do, do it with thy might." I pinned mine onto a shrinking heart.

The closing hymn was the clincher: "Take My Life, and Let It Be Consecrated." I was finished. I mentally said goodbye to those blissfully free hours and prepared myself to accept the responsibility for ten toilet roll covers, six tree ornaments, four pairs of mittens, two dozen cookies, an afternoon of sorting, an afternoon of selling, and an afternoon of clearing up at the bazaar.

Our spiritual food dispensed with, we got down to the real business of the evening. Mrs. Bellows handed out patterns for various ornaments. Mrs. Clark demonstrated some of the trickier versions. Mrs. Baine showed us some new slipper variations, and we all tried our hand at the margarine tub top angels. (Actually, mine turned out pretty well.)

You'll be pleased to know that I had several requests for the poodle pattern. Perhaps we should consider marketing these things ourselves. I bet we could think of a lot more things that could be covered by poodles: teapots, pencil holders, garbage cans, television sets—why the possibilities are endless! We could build a marketing empire based on poodles; we could start a whole new trend in home decorating; we could be as big as pink flamingos. But, I digress.

The meeting ended with a display of some of the work our members had already done. There was the usual stuff: knitted slippers, mittens, oven gloves, place mats, tea cosies—most with Santa motifs, or at least a sprinkling of holly and poinsettias. Audrey Cleary, however, had made the most beautiful wild flower stationery. She had dried flowers and pressed them between clear sheets, and then glued them onto writing paper. They were exquisite. Every one was different, and I kept thinking of how much time she had spent on each arrangement.

From Show and Tell time, we launched into a spirited discussion on pricing. Mrs. Baine always aims for the low side. "That way, we'll be sure to sell everything, and we won't be left with a lot of junk on our hands." On the other end of the scale, Mrs. Candy, our treasurer, is out to make our fortune. "People like to spend money at the bazaar. After all, everyone knows it's for a good cause. Let's take in as much as we can." Who can argue with logic like that?

In the end, the bottom line was the cost of the materials, so we priced accordingly. Two dollars worth of wool meant a two dollar ticket on the item. There was no markup for labor or skill or originality.

I put my hand in my purse to pull out the check. I'd still rather just pay the price and have my freedom.

I looked over at Audrey Cleary and wondered how she felt, having her beautiful work offered at bargain-basement prices. Without thinking, I said, "How much would your stationery be worth at a gift shop, Audrey? That is, if they paid you for your time and your skill?"

Audrey smiled at me. I noticed how tired she looked. No wonder: three children under seven, a big house, and, ever since her husband hurt his back, all the farm work to be done. How on earth had she ever found time for her handicrafts?

"I don't count time and skill," she said. She looked a little embarrassed, and I wished I'd kept my thoughts to myself. "The way I see it, they both come from the Lord, and since that's who I'm working for when I'm making things for the bazaar, well, I can hardly charge for them, can I?" She carefully tidied up her sheets of paper and, without looking at any of us, said, "I like to make things for the bazaar. I pray over each and every item, and I like to think that when someone buys something, they buy a prayer as well." She laughed softly. "For the Christmas bazaar, I always pray that the person will find Christ in their Christmas. It's kind of fun, picturing some absolute stranger benefiting from my prayer."

I put my check away, picked up my pattern for the margarine tub top angel, and came home.

Today, I started knitting the first pair of mitts. You know, Christine, it is fun, just as Audrey said. I pictured some small child receiving them, perhaps as a Christmas present, and then I prayed special things for that child. The time that I had earlier resented giving up became a time with the Lord. I was wrapped in meaningful meditation, contemplating the true meaning of Christmas, just as I had wanted to be.

I can hardly wait to start on the pink poodles—they are going to need some special prayer!

Must go now. My knitting needles call.

Love and a hug all around,

Pat

6.

WELCOME BACK,
AUTUMN

To every thing there is a season, and a time to every purpose under the heaven. —Ecclesiastes 3:1

October 1

Dear Christine,

It's started already. I've barely gotten the children back to school and my life back in post-summer order, and already some eager beaver is hurling me into the Christmas season. I received two invitations in the mail this morning, both for Christmas activities.

Yesterday at work, the list went up on the bulletin board for possible dates for the Christmas party. We were asked to make a selection before Friday so that the committee could book the hall. After Friday, we can't even be sure that the hall will be available on any date in December.

I don't want to think about Christmas yet. I don't care if we can't get a hall in December. How can I, when the trees are beginning to turn a glorious gold, there is that nip in the air, and the morning mist on the pond lingers until noon? It's autumn. It's not the time to worry about whether the blue satin dress is too tight for the office party or whether I should take those anchovy appetizers to Joan's.

It's time to savor the sight of a skein of geese threading the skies overhead; to watch the pumpkins turn golden in my garden; to drain the pool, order hay for the donkeys, and check the antifreeze in the car.

Remember that song we used to sing, "To every thing, . . . there is a season, turn, turn, turn"? Well, somehow, we've bumped this season off the calendar. We dive directly from back-to-school bargains to only-sixty-shopping-days-til-Christmas. Will someone tell me what happened to the autumn I know and love? Where did apple picking (without making apple-head dolls for Christmas bazaars); long walks in the woods (without picking up cones for Christmas wreaths); flea-market shopping (without looking for stocking stuffers); pickling, preserving, and freezing (without making up little jars for gift-giving); pressed leaves; apple cider; and the last rose of summer all go? All we have left of autumn is one lousy month—September. October and November have disappeared. Autumn has become a new season: pre-Christmas.

I overheard two women talking in the supermarket checkout line the other day. They were discussing the evening courses at our local college. One lady was saying that she had always wanted to take a ceramics course, and she was so glad that the college had finally offered one.

"But, can you believe it?" she said. "When I asked if they would be offering the course again in January, they said that it was available as a fall course only."

Her friend shook her head. Even the cashier pursed her lips and clucked in sympathy.

"Don't they realize that no one takes courses in the fall? Why, people have to get ready for Christmas. We don't have time to fritter away on evening courses when Christmas is looming just around the corner."

Several people in the line nodded in agreement.

"I think we should write them a letter; send a petition if we have to. All the courses should be offered after Christmas, when people have time to enjoy themselves."

I half expected her to whip out a petition sheet there and then. While she was at it, why not just get up a petition and wipe out autumn altogether. We could go directly from September 30 to December 1, and simply make December ninety-two days long. That should give them enough time to get ready for Christmas.

Seems to me, Chris, that there wasn't a great deal of preparation for the first Christmas. As far as I can tell, they didn't even prebook their room. By today's split-second Christmas planning, that was pretty sloppy on Joseph's part. I'm not sure that Mary spent too much time on getting ready for Christmas, either. The only folks who were doing any planning ahead were the Wise Men. Except, they didn't know exactly what it was they were planning for. I have a feeling that our office Christmas party committee would be appalled by the whole slipshod affair. Worse, if our committee ran their party like the first Christmas, they'd probably be out of a job. After all, our office is known for its great Christmas parties, and we have our reputation to protect!

All right, all right. Enough grumbling.

It's quite simple, isn't it? Autumn hasn't really gone anywhere. It's still here, still right outside my window. If I've lost it, then I've allowed it to be lost. And it's perfectly within my power to reclaim it. Which I now do! Welcome back October and November. So long Santa—see you in December, maybe.

In the meantime, I will enjoy the "now" of this season

instead of living in the worries of the next. Perhaps our removal of autumn from the calendar is one of the reasons that we find the Christmas season so harried. We haven't allowed ourselves any breathing space between summer and Christmas. When I watch the earth around me settle down for its long winter solstice, I realize that there is order in our seasons. If only we humans would take the hint and use the slowing autumn days to calm our souls and prepare spiritually for the great event of our Lord's birth. Instead, we waste these lovely days in frenzied activity, hoping that when the great day comes, we will "be ready."

Having made that momentous decision, tell me, Chris, what am I supposed to do with these invitations? Do I ignore them until December 1 (do I dare?)? Do I tear them up; call and accept right away and refuse to think about them again; write a note explaining my new position on autumn; accept but don't mark the dates on the calendar? I'm getting tired just making a decision.

Just a minute here—these are Christmas decisions we're talking about, and I have just decided that the pre-Christmas season does not begin until after autumn. Sorry folks—you'll have to wait a few months for my reply.

Chris, I feel as if a load has been rolled off my mind. I'm free to enjoy today, this season, this moment. Welcome back autumn. I've missed you.

Love and an autumnal hug,

Pat

7.

THANKSGIVING
IN DECEMBER

In every thing give thanks: for this is the will of God in Christ Jesus concerning you. —1 Thessalonians 5:18

October 12

Dear Christine,

Happy Thanksgiving to you and yours! This is easily one of my favorite holidays. It comes earlier here than to our neighbors to the south, but then, our harvest is earlier, too. I love the golden color in the air when the sun hits the poplar leaves, and I love the smell of the fruits and vegetables decorating the church, and I love the hymns we sing—"We plow the fields and scatter The good seed on the land," and I really love the fabulous meal we all share. I bet I put on an ounce for every pound of turkey I cooked! This year, I really outdid myself and baked six, count 'em, six pies: apple, pumpkin, chocolate, lemon meringue, rhubarb, and one unidentified berry pie from a bag of frozen whatever-they-weres that I found in the freezer. The general consensus was that it was possibly a boysenberry pie, but the votes were not unanimous. It was, however, delicious!

Thanksgiving always works. I look around me, and there's always something to be thankful for. Even if all the usual trappings of plenty aren't in evidence, there's my family and friends. The bottom line of it is that the Lord has always given me a roof over my head and food on my table. The "attitude of gratitude" comes easily at Thanksgiving.

I wonder if Christmas would work better in this world if we could hinge it on the tangible like we do at Thanksgiving? You know what I mean. In every church, at every children's time, on every Thanksgiving, the minister asks the kids what they are thankful for. They don't have any trouble answering him: Mommy and Daddy, their new bike, nice clothes, friends, toys, pets, chocolate bars, and Superman lunch boxes. Ask the grownups, and the answers vary only in their level of sophistication: a good home, a healthy family (or a healthy bank account), and a secure job. Sometimes they will wax eloquent on freedom of speech and the democratic process, but generally, the tangible wins the day.

If the same minister were to ask the same children what they were thankful for on Christmas Day, discounting any gifts they might be expecting under the tree, nine out of ten would be stumped for the answer. The tenth, prompted by a nearby Sunday school teacher, might mention the baby Jesus. It's hard to feel grateful for a baby that was born nearly two thousand years ago, especially if you weren't around at the time. It's much easier to list the presents under the tree!

I've been thinking a lot about that "attitude of gratitude." I think it may be what I've been missing at Christmastime. You know, when I was preparing that gargantuan feast last weekend, I wasn't feeling the least bit "poor me" as I slaved in the kitchen. I was feeling grateful for all the harvest bounty from my garden, for all the friends in my living room, and for the beauty of the autumn world outside my window. That "attitude of gratitude" made the work a kind of thanksgiving offering of my own.

I wonder if it would work the same way with Christmas. If I could truly feel grateful for the coming of Jesus to the world, wouldn't all the doing, rushing, and shopping become a part of my thanksgiving?

Thanksgiving at Christmas. Well, why not? If I can foist off an unidentifiable pie on the world, they'll hardly notice Thanksgiving in December. I think I'll work on that "attitude of gratitude" and see what happens. Keep ya posted!

Love and a thankful hug,

Pat

PS. Speaking of Thanksgiving, I give thanks every time I write to you that you are a part of my life. A special hug just for you.

P.

8.

GOODBYE JACK O'LANTERN; HELLO SANTA

*They shall ask the way to Zion with their faces thither-
ward, saying, Come, and let us join ourselves to the Lord
in a perpetual covenant that shall not be forgotten.*
—Jeremiah 50:5

November 1

Dear Christine,

Well, today is "Good-bye Jack o'Lantern, hello Santa" day! Last night I was handing out tricks and treats to the goblins at my door, and this morning I was standing ten feet deep in people waiting for the parade. The Santa Claus Parade, that is. (I've often wondered whether Santa has to fight a rush-hour crowd as the Halloween witches head home while he tries to make his way down from the North Pole.)

I know what you're thinking. "How come she was at the Santa Claus Parade when it isn't December yet?" No, I didn't forget. I'm still enjoying autumn, which, I might add, has yet another month to run. It's just that it's difficult to explain to children that they can't watch a parade because their mother has decided to opt out of this world's Christmas. Of course, the fact that Nathan's scout group was on one of the floats had nothing to do with it. Much.

The parade was predictable in every way: float with dancing snowmen; float with candy-cane forest; float with Santa's workshop; float with singing toys; all interspersed with high school marching bands, police bands, highland pipers, majorettes, and clowns. I bet we could take all the Santa Claus parades in the country, jumble them up, plunk them down just anywhere, and no one would know the difference. Except of course, our parade always has a live chicken in a broken-down baby carriage. I understand it's some kind of tradition here in Spencerville. However, chicken aside, a Santa Claus Parade is always the same.

We watched it all go by as our noses turned red and our toes became numb. Cherith was talking hot chocolate at the lunch counter in Woolworth's, and by the time the umpteenth band had passed by, I was inclined to think she had a good idea. Finally, the finale: Santa Claus, complete with sleigh and eight (count 'em) reindeer, dispersing largess in the way of candy canes to the waiting multitudes. "Jingle Bells" blared from four speakers, and "Ho, Ho, Ho!" echoed over our heads. He was, as usual, magnificent in all his red-suited glory.

I was all set to make a dash for Woolworth's and beat the crowds, but Cherith held me back until Santa had passed by. I'm glad she did.

Right behind Santa's flashy sleigh, walking quietly, looking neither left nor right—in fact, totally oblivious to the screaming crowds—were a man and a woman dressed in biblical style. She was seated on a small donkey and looked very pregnant. There was no music, not even a Christmas carol. In fact, it was as if they walked in their own small world of silence—or of peace. They were so inconspicuous that I doubt if many in the crowd even noticed them. But those of us who did felt a lump grow in our throats and tears sting our eyes. Somehow, it was so fitting that these two should walk quietly in the wake of the noise and commotion of our

Christmas, bringing with them a sense of the first Christmas.

Later, while sipping hot chocolate at the lunch counter, I found out that the local Gospel church had slipped the small group in behind Santa, much to the annoyance of the parade organizers. In fact, the organizers had tried to keep them out, but there is no law that says you cannot walk behind Santa's sleigh.

I wonder if there's a law that says the Santa Claus Parade has to come as early as possible in order to get people out shopping as soon as possible. Some organizer somewhere must have realized that you couldn't have Santa Claus come before Halloween, but there's nothing to stop him coming the day after. That gives people two frenzied months in which to shop and prepare. Better still, it gives television advertisers two whole months to brainwash our children. Two whole months of "Jingle Bells" and "Silent Night" and "G.I. Joe." Two months . . .

Better not to think about it. Better to remind myself that I'm not playing this year. We may have seen Santa Claus this morning, but as far as I'm concerned, he can go back to the North Pole and read his mail. As for me, I'm going to be like those two people behind his sleigh. I'm going to go on my own pilgrimage; one that will hopefully take me to the same manger that awaits them. In the meantime, I have another month of autumn to enjoy.

By the way, Chris, I've received three more invitations, and I've put them in the pile with the others. This is fun, but I'm a little concerned that no one has called me for an answer. Can it be that I'm just a check mark on their guest list? Well, then so be it. This is one check mark that will have to wait for another month.

I've finished knitting all the mitts. Now I'm on to the poodle covers. I'm having trouble visualizing a prayer for the person who buys them. I think I'll just stick with some general blessings and try not to get too specific. Mitts were easier.

Love and a hug,

Pat

PS. Remember my calligraphy course? I forgot to tell you that I never made it back after the first class. I was sick the next week, and the week after that, Nathan had to go to a cub meeting, and by then, I figured I'd never catch up anyhow. This means I'll have to go back to my previous Christmas card practices—grab a box at the last moment and send them airmail. Wait! I can't believe I just wrote that! That's just the kind of thing I promised myself I wouldn't do this year. But what should I do instead? I'm not writing Christmas cards in November—it's still autumn. Never mind, I'm sure I'll think of something.

9.

THE SIREN CALL
OF THE CHRISTMAS MONSTER

There is therefore now no condemnation to them which are in Christ Jesus, who walk not after the flesh, but after the Spirit. —Romans 8:1

November 15

Dear Christine,

It's no good. There's still two weeks of official autumn left, but I'm slowly being sucked into the gaping maw of the Christmas Monster. Everywhere I go, he waits for me, lurking behind the plastic Christmas trees, hiding under the displays of Christmas wrapping paper, waiting to ambush me when I am least prepared to fight off his advances. Even the grocery store isn't safe—he's sitting on the shelves of candy, smirking from the bins of nuts and oranges, and most of all, blatantly calling to me from the loudspeakers that insist on interspersing the fifteen-minute produce specials with "O Holy Night."

It's his message that gets to me, a siren call that is irresistible to my sense of responsibility. "Only twenty-five more shopping days until Christmas." Suddenly, my whole life becomes compressed into twenty-five days. Can I do it? Can I get it all done if I start this very second and don't stop? Twenty-five days! Why, that's barely enough time to stuff a turkey, let alone create a Christmas that my family will speak of with awe and reverence for years to come.

As a wife and mother, I have a *responsibility* to make sure that Christmas is wonderful. It is *up to me* to bring

Christmas into the hearts of my family. It is *my duty* to give everyone a memorable day. And I've only got twenty-five days left to do it in!

No wonder I feel the adrenalin surge when the Christmas Monster whispers "only twenty-five days" into my ear. Despite all my resolutions and protests, somewhere deep inside me is the notion that everyone else's Christmas rests with me. If I don't make it happen, no one will. Maybe that's why the faces I see racing frantically from store to store are usually female faces.

No, no, Chris. This isn't my woman's lib lecture. I promise. It's simply a statement that we have been conditioned to believe that the female of the species is responsible for the quality of Christmas. I mean, let's face it—there aren't a whole lot of sons and husbands out there baking up a storm, wrapping up Great Aunt Joan's present and mailing it to Australia (on time), dragging the kids to see Santa Claus, sewing angels' wings on the backs of the junior choir, or driving twenty miles out of their way to get a Super-Star Barbie complete with six glamorous outfits.

Chris, do I see a nod of agreement? Of course I do. You know exactly what I'm talking about. Every woman does. Where is it written that Christmas is the woman's responsibility? And how did it become so graven in stone that we all bow to the inevitability of our responsibility? Now, there's a profound thought . . . "the inevitability of our responsibility." That might make an interesting consciousness-raising topic some day.

So, having said all that, I'm back to two weeks left of autumn and a Christmas Monster whispering in my ear that it's all going down the tubes this year if I don't pull myself together and do something about it! The dilemma lies in my decision not to *do* things this year. The end result, of course, is an overwhelming sense of guilt that I'm letting everyone down by sticking to my resolution.

Not that anyone near and dear to me has even hinted that they feel let down. They don't need to; my own guilt does it for them.

I never realized that opting out of "Christmassyness" was going to be so difficult. I thought I could just sit back and let it flow around me. Unfortunately, what is flowing around me is the rest of the world's version of "getting ready for Christmas," and I'm beginning to feel a little bit like a salmon swimming upstream—to mix a metaphor or two.

Do you remember the Bible study we did years ago on guilt and redemption that sounded a lot heavier than it actually was? Remember how excited we were about the notion that the only person who can make you feel guilty is yourself? That guilt was a purely inward emotion? That we could choose to feel guilty or not to feel guilty? That our guilt was only a symptom of our own perceived shortcomings? Well, I wonder if this Christmas guilt I'm feeling is just a symptom of what I think I should do rather than what I know I want to do?

Hmmm . . . a little food for thought there. Especially since I am a past master of guilt. I even feel guilty if I use the last sheet on the toilet paper roll! (No, I am not going to get into my poodle cover exploits at this point!)

Well, I'm going to choose not to feel guilty. So there! I've got two more wonderful weeks of autumn to go, and I'm not going to let any insidious, little voice try to turn that into a countdown of shopping days.

I feel better already.

By the way, I started knitting those sweaters again. It's a darn sight more comfortable to do in the cooler weather, and it's somehow very much in rhythm with the season as I click off row after row. Most importantly, I'm enjoying the knitting. I haven't told any of the gang that I'm back on the job—this way the sweaters will come as a complete surprise under the tree. And, if I do get fed up and chuck the whole lot back into the grocery bag, no one will ever know how close they came to having a hand-knit sweater. The pressure is off now, and I don't feel as if I have to finish them. I don't have to prove anything to anyone.

My Christmas mail pile is growing daily. I didn't realize how popular we were! It's going to be fun sorting through them all. It's almost like having a birthday—all those surprise occasions just waiting to be enjoyed.

Wish we could spend some of them with you and yours. Hugs all around.

Love,

Pat

PS. Could you send me that pattern for the knitted doggie coat? I just may get completely carried away, and I want to be prepared. I promise that I will not knit little somethings for the chickens, although I can't say that I won't do a muffler or two for my favorite cats.

P.

10.

WHERE ANGELS FEAR
TO TREAD

*Stand ye in the ways, and see, and ask for the old paths,
where is the good way, and walk therein, and ye shall find
rest for your souls.* —Jeremiah 6:16

November 22

Dear Christine,

Please don't read the date on this letter. I have advanced the Christmas season by approximately seven days, or to be brutal about it, I have just chopped a whole week off of autumn.

As of ten o'clock this morning, I am now officially in charge of the Sunday School Christmas Concert. Did I hear you gasp? Was it in horror or surprise or joy? A little of all three, perhaps. That's certainly how I'm feeling now that I have had time to digest the big news.

Let me tell you what happened. We had a meeting of all the Sunday school teachers this morning on the subject of the Christmas concert. It was unavoidable. You know there is no way that I could have convinced anyone to wait another week or two before discussing the concert. As it was, they were pretty nervous about the shortness of planning time.

Anyway, we plodded through countless books with Christmas plays and pageants and dramas. We looked at monologues and pantomimes and comedies. We discussed props and sets and costumes. We listed and totaled and catalogued, and in the end, the whole thing boiled down to two considerations: how many characters would be needed and how many lines they would have to learn.

On these criteria, a play was chosen that had enough characters to guarantee everyone a part and enough lines to guarantee everyone something to say. (That guaranteed that every parent would come out and we would have a full house for the concert!)

The chosen play, however, was fairly complicated, from costumes that were supposed to portray the middle ages (I suspect in the Robin Hood mood), to sets that required three complete changes. In all, it was going to be a mammoth undertaking. I said nothing. It was, after all, still November.

The rehearsal dates were set out. If we pushed hard and scheduled meetings twice a week and every Sunday afternoon, we could get the whole thing together in time for the concert on December 16. That is, of course, if we all pitched in and spent a few extra nights putting together costumes and sets. I still said nothing.

And then, someone (I wish I knew who so I could suitably thank her) suggested that Nathan would make the perfect narrator. I looked at the play. I looked at the narrator's part—line after line, paragraph after paragraph—and I looked at the narrator's costume, "that of a king of the period, preferably in velvet with gold trim, complete with crown and complementing jewels," and I saw it all before me. Endless evenings of "Nathan, just pronounce it the way I'm saying it," and "Nathan, hold still while I pin this in place," and "Nathan, you have to know those lines by next Thursday," and "Nathan, where did you put your crown?"

I said something.

Actually, Chris, what I said was, "Forget this play. Let me do the Christmas concert this year. I know of a play that needs no rehearsals, no sets, no lines, no narrators, and no costumes. Leave the whole thing to me."

Needless to say, there wasn't a great deal of opposition to my suggestion. Actually, there wasn't a nay in the room. Of course, I did have a little ace up my sleeve. I had that Christmas pageant I saw in Newfoundland years ago. (I've enclosed a copy for you.) Glance over it. Simple. Easy to do. No rehearsals. Beautiful message. Most importantly, I don't have to think about it again until December 1 at the earliest.

So, here I am, the Chief Executive Officer of the Official Sunday School Christmas Concert. I should be feeling put-upon or, at the very least, martyred, but I don't. That's because I'm into that "attitude of gratitude" I was telling you about earlier. For once and for all, I'd like to help it happen at the Christmas concert. Usually, by the time the great night comes, we're all too exhausted from preparations to enjoy the performance, and the kids are so strung out and tense with line-learning and rehearsals that they walk through the whole thing like robots. Somewhere in the midst of the candy canes and tinsel we miss the purpose for the concert. It's supposed to be part of a glorious birthday celebration, but it becomes an endurance race.

I know there are always glimpses of glory in the midst of it all, those priceless little moments when we see the beauty of Christmas in the innocence of a young child's face. But it always ends up with S. Claus and company doling out gifts and candy. The manger is pushed out of the way to make room for Santa's sack, and our last memory of the evening is "Jingle Bells" and "Ho, Ho, Ho."

This year, I promise, it's going to be different. This year is going to be fun. Most of all, Chris, this year is going to be my gift to the Sunday school.

I can't wait to get at it. First notice will go out next week: "Please ask all junior children to bring a brown paper bag to Sunday school. The bag should be large enough to fit over the child's head." That should give them all something to wonder over.

I'll talk to the minister and brief him on his part. Believe me, if he can't manage it, he must have been sleeping every Christmas for the past twenty years! And I'll talk to our choir director. One hymn isn't too much to ask from the senior choir.

But not until December 1. Nothing Christmassy is going to happen until December 1. I've saved autumn once again. I wonder if they'll ever put up a plaque in my honor: "The Lady Who Saved Autumn."

Well, I didn't save it completely. I have to confess, Christine, that I actually (how can I put this delicately, so as not to shock you even further?), with intention and aforethought, bought two Christmas gifts. And mailed them. There. I feel much better. Confession is good for the soul.

I didn't really have any choice. The deadline for mailing overseas parcels is tomorrow. To be honest, I enjoyed shopping for just two small gifts. My mind wasn't all cluttered up with a gift list for everyone within shouting distance. And I promise, I won't slip again. Christmas gifts are the furthest thing from my mind for the next week.

I have another confession to make. Deep inside, I'm beginning to feel that warm glow that signals the beginning of the season. The calendar may say November, but my heart is beginning to say Advent. This year, I'm going to preserve the glow and not allow it to be damped down by frazzled nerves and short tempers.

Come along Advent.

Love to all, and a hug to you,

Pat

PS. Nearly forgot to tell you. I have finished all the sweaters. And all the poodle toilet roll covers and all the slippers. The bazaar is next Thursday. Stay tuned.

11.

BAZAAR
HAPPENINGS

We have this treasure in earthen vessels, that the excellency of the power may be of God, and not of us.

—2 Corinthians 4:7

November 29

Dear Christine,

Hi! A quick note to you so that you can see this lovely notepaper I bought at today's bazaar. Isn't it truly beautiful? I thought you'd like this one with the violets and ferns on it. I wonder what prayer Audrey put in with the package I bought.

The bazaar was a resounding success. Our poodles sold out! I still think we should consider a franchise operation, Chris. How about "Poodle Doodles" for a name? Or "Oodles of Poodles"?

Love,

Pat

PS. Something is happening! I enjoyed the bazaar today, especially watching people buying Audrey's notepaper and my mittens, knowing that they were buying some special prayers as well. Talk about heavenly treasure in earthen vessels!

P.

12.

DON'T TRAMPLE MY TRADITIONS

He leadeth me beside the still waters. He restoreth my soul. —Psalm 23:2–3

First Sunday in Advent

Dear Christine,

It's the first Sunday in Advent today. On every first Sunday for the past ten years, I have spent the better part of the afternoon, sometimes in rain, sleet, snow, or hail, looking for pinecones and bits of twigs and dried leaves and what-have-you to make an Advent wreath. In fact, I think you and I have spent some of those Sunday afternoons together creating wreaths from an incredible array of weeds and nuts. The wreaths always looked great, but what a mess! White glue and cotton batting, pulverized leaves and broken branches, not to mention bits of glitter, tinsel, and candle wax all over the kitchen counter. After that, as you know, every Advent evening we bring out the wreath, light a candle, sing a hymn, read a verse, and the tradition carries on.

Despite the mess and bother, it really was a lovely tradition, wasn't it? Notice the past tense. It hasn't been so lovely for the past couple of years. My darling children, approaching teenagerhood, have become too "sophisticated" for such traditions. Last year was the pits. After the first Sunday evening, when Nathan wouldn't read the verse, Cherith couldn't light a candle, and they were both profoundly embarrassed when I started to sing the carols, I began to think that maybe we had outgrown our tradition. I was convinced of it when they suggested we should do it later because there was a good program on TV. When later did come, it was time for homework and then a bath, and after that they had to make lunches. Excuses, excuses.

This year, this morning in fact, I decided to drop the tradition. After all, it was pretty meaningless when it played second fiddle to a television program! And the fact that there has been a steady downpour with a chill wind from the north hasn't heightened my enthusiasm for a brisk walk through the back forty looking for pine-cones. So I didn't make the wreath this afternoon. I didn't think anyone would even notice.

I was wrong. Chris, you wouldn't believe the carry-ings-on around here when the kids realized that the wreath wasn't made and we weren't going to do our usual candle-lighting ceremony. Shock! Horror! Dismay!

"But we always do it!"

"It's Advent."

"I like lighting the candle."

"It was my turn to read."

There are times, Chris, when I think I'm living with a family of loony-tunes. Could these be the same children who for the past two years have shown utter disdain for my little tradition? Now, when it seems to be in jeopardy, it has become a vital part of their pre-Christmas celebrations!

Of course, you know what I did. I cobbled together a makeshift wreath with some leftover bits from the Christmas ornament box and a few boughs from the cedar tree on the lawn, and topped it off with the only available candles we could find, which, to everyone's disgust, were blue and not the usual white.

We had our traditional ceremony. And traditionally, Nathan acted silly, Cherith giggled, they both snickered when I sang, and we all heaved a small sigh of relief when we had finished.

So why carry on? you're asking. Because I have decided that there must be something of intrinsic value in our traditions. Why else would those world-weary children of mine still want to carry on the tradition? Deep inside, in some small place in their hearts, well hidden from the outside world, and, perhaps, even from their own consciousness, there must be a part of their spirit that is warmed and touched by Advent. Not just by the tradition, but by the hearing of the Christmas story, the singing of the old carols, and even by the symbolic lighting of the Advent candles. And I bet a hundred wreaths that those same children will carry on the tradition in their families. I wish I could be a fly on the wall the first time their children decide that something better is on television! It will serve them right, I say. (Someone once said that grandchildren are a parent's only revenge.)

My Christmas concert leadership is going well. I keep getting calls from worried parents wondering what they should be doing for the Sunday school concert. I'm not sure they believe me when I say, "Nothing." The notices have gone out for necessary materials. I've booked the junior choir gowns, the senior choir's voices, and the minister. Our one and only rehearsal is still nearly two weeks away. I picked up an old fur coat at the rummage sale that should round out the costumes nicely. Nothing left to do. Ta Dah!

I'm still open for suggestions for Christmas cards. I think I have about two weeks left before it's all over for another year. Remember, we're looking for meaningful, easy, personal, and fast.

Am I getting caught up in this world's Christmas? I don't think so. I definitely don't feel the usual pressures around me. I've opened all our invitations and booked them on the calendar. Said yes to some and no to others (notably those looking for someone to say grace over the turkey). The bazaar is behind me; the Sunday school concert is well in hand; the sweaters are all knitted; I even have the Advent wreath made! Guess I'll sit back and hum a carol or two. I may even start picking up a gift here and there. Not a marathon shopping trip; just as and when I see something.

This is the first time in many years that I've really felt that I am taking part in Advent. In the church, it's supposed to be a time for preparation, but unfortunately, I've always gotten caught up in the wrong kind of preparation. There's a part of the service that says we're supposed to be preparing our hearts and minds for the coming of our Lord. That kind of preparation usually calls for a little peace and contemplation, hard things to find in December.

Thinking back to our Advent wreath this evening, I realize that most of our traditions provide a moment of peace and contemplation that we have nowhere else in our day. Even if it's for only ten minutes once a week, it is a time when we consciously start preparing our hearts and minds. Could it be that even my poppets recognize the value of those minutes at this time of the year?

Next year, I'll have the wreath ready. Don't trample my traditions, guys. Even an opted-out mother needs a little order in her life.

Love and hugs all around,

Pat

P.S. Loved your idea for the tails in the Sunday school concert. Shouldn't be too hard to pull off (or should I say, put on?).

13.

AND THE WINNER IS . . .

What things were gain to me, those I counted loss for Christ. —Philippians 3:7

December 10

Dear Christine,

Greetings from the Queen of the Cookie Sheets! I have just finished a battle to the death in the kitchen. It was touch and go for awhile, but in the end, the forces of Pat triumphed. Mind you, I had to wipe out an entire battalion of cookie cutters to do it!

After the kids' reaction to my near scuttling of the Advent wreath, I didn't dare wipe the annual baking session from the calendar. We assembled our forces at the crack of doom last Saturday morning (and you know how fond I am of anything that happens in the A.M.; the way I see it, if God had wanted us to see the dawn, it would have been scheduled later in the day!). Raisins, nuts, colored sprinkles, silver balls, icing sugar . . . we were ready to do battle. A brief foray into the cookbooks produced a foolproof strategy: two batches of sugar cookies, some gingernuts, and a pan or two of short-bread. With any luck, we'd be baked out by noon, and the day (and I) would still be young.

All went well until the opposing forces launched a surprise attack. Cherith found the perfect recipe for gingerbread men, and could we make some? Sure, why not? The spirit was upon me, and I felt we could conquer all.

Then, Gerald requested some of the cookies he remembered from his youth in Holland. His description
sounded something like a recipe I remembered seeing
in one of my church cookbooks. It was finally located
but required a few ingredients we didn't have on hand.
Gerald volunteered to go to the store. Nathan wanted to
go with him. Cherith and I stayed behind to hold the
line on the eggbeaters.

I went out to feed the chickens and left Cherith in
charge. She turned on the Saturday cartoons. We lost a
pan of gingerbread men. A short, meaningful service
was held before their commitment to the depths of the
garbage pail.

That small battle may have been lost, but there was
still a war to win. We retaliated by baking up two
batches of sugar cookies, cut out painstakingly in every
conceivable Christmas shape. They came out of the
oven delicately browned and perfect in every way. We
slipped them on the cookie racks to cool. I started to mix
up some colored icing sugar. The phone rang.

When I returned, Splodgy-puss was wearing a
Cheshire-cat grin. Splodgy loves sweet things. He'd
polished off a whole rack of cookies, and those he
couldn't manage, he thoughtfully dropped on the floor
for the dog. There was, however, still one rack of cookies
relatively untouched. (I say relatively because I had no
intention of inspecting them closely, or of speculating
on whether Splodgy had sampled a few of them before
heading for the second rack). Cherith and I decorated
them with an artistic flair that would have won prizes in
any art gallery. Well, why not? There were only two

dozen to do, and unlike most Christmas baking ses-
sions when you get so bored with putting those slip-
pery little silver balls right in the middle of the star
cookies, we had hardly enough cookies to really get our
artistic teeth into. (Unlike Splodgy and the dog!)

The shortbread was mixed, baked, and packed in tins
to mature. Shortbread is usually uneventful, and at this
point in the morning, now waning rapidly, I was glad of
any uneventuality.

Cherith and I whipped up another squadron of gingerbread men, and while she was giving them currant
eyesight, I rolled out another sheet of jam jams. I began
to savor the sweet taste of victory. (Not to mention some
of the cookie samples. It is not true that I always make
some cookies a little funny looking so I will have an
excuse to eat them.) The male contingent returned with
fresh supplies. Heartened by our small victories, we
headed confidently back into the battle.

Defeat was swift and bitter. Whatever they were that
Gerald remembered from his youth were not repro-
ducable in my kitchen. The first batch were like hard
little brown marbles. The chickens loved them. I made
the second batch a little larger and added more liquid.
They spread into one gooey mass on the cookie sheet
that had to be scraped off. The dog thought they were
pretty good. The third batch (yes, Chris, third) looked
fine. They were round and dark and their egg-white
surface was shiny and cracked. However, somewhere in
the heat of the moment, I had put in curry powder
instead of ginger. Even the dog wouldn't try them.
(Note to all cooks: never bake anything while suffering

from a head cold. The nose is a vital piece of baking equipment!)

As if sensing our imminent defeat, the family quietly slunk away to other interests. I cleaned up the debris of the battle, packed away the cookies, and called it a day. Then I called Ted, the baker in town and who just happens to be Dutch, and asked him to make a batch of Gerald's cookies. He knew exactly what I was talking about and was glad to oblige.

Ha! I win!

"No fair," you say. Not so. In past years, I would have spent hours and hours trying to bake a lifelong supply of Christmas cookies. It was part of that guilt trip I was on, the part that said it wasn't a "real" Christmas if I didn't have at least five cookie tins full of home-baked goodies. Bah, humbug!

Do you realize that you can buy a tin full of Christmas cookies from any corner store and that the cost is considerably less than that of the ingredients you'd need to make them, not to mention the lost hours of frustration? But what about family togetherness? the Christmas monster cries. What about it? I reply. Usually, six hours into the baking battle, my temper is enough to make any family member wish that they could get together with me some other time, some other place. I suspect they'd also like some other mother to get together with. And who can blame them?

But not this year. As soon as I realized we were losing the battle, I opted out. I left it all behind me, and we went skiing. Ted can fill the rest of my cookie tins. You see, Chris, I really did win.

It all boils back down to the reason for doing things. If

the reason is simply from a sense of guilt, then there's no point in *doing*. It's like my knitting. As long as I was knitting from a sense of guilt (mixed in with a liberal dose of martyrdom), then there was no joy in it. If I'm baking Christmas cookies because I'll feel guilty if I don't, there isn't much love baked in with them. And after all, isn't love the reason for the season in the first place?

I sent six Christmas cards out yesterday. Did it the easy way. Went into the corner drugstore, picked out six nice cards, addressed them to my faraway friends (that is, anyone I don't see at least once a year), and mailed them off. I bet the whole procedure took less than half an hour. Of course, I still have the rest of the world to worry about. No, I'm not going to worry about it. Something will turn up. Any ideas?

Speaking of ideas, I tried some of those you suggested for costumes. Brilliant. Perhaps you've missed your calling in life. Have you ever considered heading for Hollywood and costume design?

The Sunday school superintendent hinted very strongly that I had better know what I'm doing. O ye of little faith!

Here's a big, pink-iced, silver-ball-trimmed hug from me to all of you.

Pat

P.S. Your Christmas card is on the way, and not by courier. It's been more than a year since I last saw you. Much more than a year, and far too long.

14.

PLASTIC
CHRISTMAS

In him was life; and the life was the light of men.
—John 1:4

December 15

Dear Christine,

It's very late. I can't sleep. The elastic on my eye patch is pinching me, and my eye is itching like crazy. Got your attention, didn't I?

Yes, I'm one of the walking wounded, a gruesome reminder to the rest of the world that this Christmas business is a lot more than just fun and games.

It all started so innocently. We decided to head for the back forty and cut ourselves a Christmas tree. Since we have about twenty-five acres of various evergreens, there was no problem with supply. Demand was another story. I wanted a big tree, Mother wanted a bushy tree, Cherith wanted a tall tree, and Nathan wanted a tree that wouldn't be too heavy to drag home. It took us several hours to find just the right one. We cut it down without incident. Needless to say, I wasn't allowed to handle the ax, given my penchant for cutting off bits of my anatomy when using any sharp instrument. We slung the tree onto the toboggan and dragged it home. At the front door, it became obvious that we had picked a tree considerably taller and wider than any area in our home, but a little judicious pruning solved the problem.

Now, Chris, you know I don't believe that inanimate objects express emotions, but I am convinced that that tree did not appreciate being pruned any further. It was with malice aforethought that it whipped its longest branch back just as we pulled it through the front door and smacked me squarely in the face. It raised several red welts and caused my eye to water.

"Water" is a polite way of describing a constant running stream of tears from a stinging, burning eyeball. I decided to ignore the pain. After all, it was time to decorate the Christmas tree, and I didn't want to spoil the fun.

I have to admit, though, it wasn't much fun decorating the tree with only one eye. In the end, I settled for handing stuff to the waiting hands and generally directing the proceedings. My eye got worse. It began to gently swell, and finally, I had to admit there was a problem.

In the emergency ward of our local hospital, the doctor scraped out several bits of pine needle and bark. He was not amused when I told him that I was attacked by an irate Christmas tree.

"Get a plastic one," he growled. "Live trees are just a nuisance. Dirty, messy things."

He was right, of course. But all wrong, too.

The way I see it, Chris, nearly everything else in our world is plastic. In fact, Christmas is slowly becoming a plastic celebration. There's plastic holly and plastic ornaments, plastic tablecloths and plastic wreaths, plastic angels and even plastic stars. I'm sure before the century is out, someone will have invented plastic turkeys for Christmas dinner!

If we're not careful, the true meaning of Christmas will become just as lifeless as the plastic manger scene on the mantle. There'll be no true spirit left; no real love, no abiding peace, no abounding joy. In its place, we'll have hollow laughter, false gaiety, and shallow fellowship. When I see the people around me who are determined to "enjoy" a season whose only spirit is liquid, I feel a deep sense of sorrow at their loss.

I'll keep my real tree, dangerous or not, if for no other reason than to remind me that the manger at Bethlehem was probably dirty and messy, too, and that, no doubt, the innkeeper felt that the whole affair was a nuisance. But isn't that the reality of life itself? How sad if we give up the dirt and mess and nuisance for the safety of a plastic world. We may then be safe from the harms of this world, but we're also immune to its best emotions—like love.

No doubt, I'll have this eye patch to keep on reminding me long after the tree has left its needles behind on my carpet. Captain Bligh bids you goodnight. All I need to complete the picture is a trusty blade and wooden leg.

Scratch that thought about the wooden leg. Who knows what revenge the tree is plotting now!

Blink, blink. Hug, hug.

Pat

PS. The concert is tomorrow night. Pray for the one-eyed director!

15.

PARDON ME,
YOUR HALO IS SLIPPING

The angel said unto them, Fear not: for, behold, I bring you good tidings of great joy, which shall be to all people.
—Luke 2:10

December 17

Dear Christine,

I've been practicing my speech. "On behalf of the Sunday school, I am honored to accept the Golden Halo Award for the best Christmas concert of the year." Yes, we did it. Pulled it off without a hitch. Had fun. And left 'em without a dry eye in the house. (Which, by the way, was packed, despite the fact that no one had any lines to say.)

I remember the first time we did this particular pageant. It came about simply because no one in the Newfoundland outport church had ever thought about having a Christmas concert. With only a week to go, no costumes, no supplies, and no script, we had to improvise. It worked there, and it worked again last night.

The senior choir sang beautifully. I knew that one carol wasn't asking too much. And even for the 152nd time this week, "Silent Night" still had the power to bring tears to my eyes. The minister read the story from Luke. As I suspected, after twenty years of practice, he had it word-perfect. Every single child had a part, and not one complained about being a shepherd!

Your ideas for the costumes were great. We got them to dress in brown or black tops and bottoms, and all we had to do was add a few bits and pieces. You've no idea how far one fur coat will go towards embellishing a band of village herdsmen (aka the shepherds). We just wrapped blankets around Mary and Joseph. After all, it was the middle of winter and pretty nippy in the barn. Once we had the angels dressed in the junior choir tops, we gave them silver tinsel halos. What a sight!

Of course, the little kids stole the show. Every one had made their paper-bag animal mask last week. There was everything from raccoons to skunks to deer. The frayed rope tails worked well, and we used rag mops for the bushier variety. You would have loved your little woodland birds—their cardboard tails were lovely.

The finale was just as touching as I remembered. Everyone was set on the stage . . . angels, kings, shepherds, and M and J. The choir hummed the tune, and one of the older boys beat a drum. Out from every corner, the little wild creatures crept up onto the stage. What the kids on stage and the audience didn't know was that we had a real baby in the manger (courtesy of Martha, who thoughtfully gave birth just a month earlier). There was a collective gasp as they glimpsed the child wrapped in furs. Nothing could ever better illustrate the true wonder of Christmas than that moment. I don't know how everyone else felt, but my one good eye suddenly wasn't much good for seeing.

The best part of the evening was how people reacted when they realized that the Christmas concert was simply the story retold—no lights, no glitter, no glitz, no bells and whistles—just the story. I'm sure everyone had that same flash of memory that I did: a memory of other concerts in other times. I remembered being seven years old, and true to form, was chosen for

Joseph, not Mary. I was feeling a little put out just
because I didn't have the requisite long curls necessary
for Mary's part. My face was covered in a horse-hair
beard that itched like crazy. But my negative feelings
were lost at the moment when I suddenly realized that I
was part of something far bigger than a bunch of kids on
the stage.

I think everyone at the concert had a similar memory:
perhaps of being a shepherd in Dad's bathrobe or an
angel with wings that wouldn't stay on or even of being
Mary. The story didn't need any fancy trimmings—it
had a power of its own.

You're not going to believe this, Chris, but we didn't
invite S. Claus and company to the concert! Instead, we
got our kings to hand out bags of nuts and fruit to every
child. After all, the precedent for handing out gifts was
set by the Three Kings in the first place.

After that, we sang carols, lots of them. Everyone had
a chance to sing their favorite, and we persuaded some
of our better singers to give us a solo or two. It was like
one large, happy family gathered around the piano in
the parlor. Isn't that the way it's supposed to be?

You know, Chris, I suspect that deep down, people
long to return to the simpler pleasures of life, like a sing-
song with family and friends. Unfortunately, we've
been led to believe that we have to compete with our
electronic world, and the Sunday school Christmas concert should be at least as spectacular as the latest rock
video. Yet, if we see the concert as a simple get-together
of Christians celebrating their Savior's birthday, the
whole emphasis changes. The way I see it, we're already inundated with Christmas "specials" on every

television channel, and we don't need more of the same at church. We had fun last night. There were no tears, no tantrums, no frayed tempers, and best of all, everyone felt involved in the celebration. The Golden Halo Award is as good as ours!

On the not-so-wonderful front, I have to admit that I have failed miserably. I haven't sent out any Christmas cards, and they're pouring (well, flowing fairly steadily) in here. There's only a week left until Christmas, and short of the old courier trick, I don't know how I'm going to pull it off. I knew I should have stuck with that calligraphy course. I'm sure that when I die, someone will write my epitaph, "She was full of good intentions." Someday, I'll learn the secret of turning an intention into an accomplishment, and I'll market it to all the rest of us good intenders and make my fortune.

I'm still open for ideas on the Christmas card front. Surely there is a simple way of wishing people the joys of the season.

Must go. One week left, and I do have some shopping to do. So far, so good. The glow is still there.

The Great One-Eyed Director sends you a hug.

Pat

PS. Did I mention that they asked me to run the whole shebang next year? We'll think about it later, say next December. No point in rushing the season, is there?

P.

16.

BORN
TO SHOP

*When they had opened their treasures, they presented
unto him gifts; gold, and frankincense, and myrrh.*
—Matthew 2:11

Next Day

This is the first time this season that I have wished there really was a Santa Claus. Then I could relax and let someone else worry about getting gifts, wrapping them and putting them under the tree. After all, that's supposed to be his job, isn't it?

I can only presume that this world got into the gift-giving business because they had someone else in mind who they expected to do the job. That's why Santa was invented in the first place. The countless hours we spend rushing from store to store only attest to a fact I have always known: there is no such thing as Santa Claus. If there were, I wouldn't have spent the better part of today doing exactly what I had decided not to do: that is, rushing, buying, and more rushing.

I thought I had this present business under control. I've been picking up a few gifts here and there; I've got knitted sweaters for everyone, even for the dog; I gave the kids money and sent them shopping for gifts for their teachers (I sure hope Cherith's teacher has always wanted long red fingernails); and I mailed off my small parcel to England a month ago. Theoretically, I shouldn't have a thing to worry about.

However, theory didn't take into account that sudden surge of the "guilts" that hits everyone just before Christmas. You know the feeling: "Did I get enough presents for the kids? Maybe I should have bought that scarf for Mother. Do the neighbors still expect presents from us? Is it too late to pick up something for the mailman?" I know who's responsible for these guilts. It's that horrible Christmas Monster, whispering that I haven't bought enough, that people will be disappointed in me.

Despite all my good intentions, the monster got me. Out I rushed, checkbook in hand, and in three hours, I reached the lowest possible ebb of Christmas gloom. Only the dregs remained on the store shelves, and I certainly wasn't going to find a Silly-Sally Teen Pop-Up Pillow, much less a Super-Sonic-Boom Radio/Microphone Combo. It didn't take long for me to realize that I wasn't going to find anything on anyone's list. But I kept on searching. Desperately, I raced from store to store, oblivious to the pitying looks of the clerks. They knew a guilt-ridden shopper when they saw one!

At the end of three hours, I had spent far more money than I ever intended for stuff that I wouldn't ordinarily look at. I can only plead temporary insanity. My one consolation is that it didn't last any longer than three hours. I have known some Christmas shoppers who suffer from the guilts for weeks on end. No amount of buying seems to still the insidious little voice that keeps telling them it's not enough.

Oh, I'll wrap up all the stuff I bought today and put it under the tree, but my heart isn't really in it. I even bought Christmas wrapping paper—so much for my plan to stick to paper bags. All in all, I'm feeling pretty depressed right now. I think I've been caught, and I'm not sure how it happened. Whether it was the sight of so many other crazed shoppers that spurred me on or a deep, unacknowledged suspicion that I was opting out of this world's Christmas for purely selfish reasons, I don't know. I just know that, for three mad hours, I was *doing* and not *being*.

When did we start to measure the quality of our Christmas joy by how many gifts we give or get? Jesus only got three gifts for his birthday, and did he look around to see where the rest were? Did Mary think that perhaps she should rush out and buy something in return? Did Joseph put the Kings' names down for next year's list? Of course not. Even the idea is ludicrous. But we do it.

Must go and wrap some gifts. In jolly Santa Claus paper. With red ribbon and bows. And a sprig of plastic holly. Bah, humbug!

Pat

Much, Much Later: This has been a long day. I should be in bed, but I wanted to let you know that something very special has happened. I went off and started wrapping the gifts. My mood was anything but Christmassy.

I got out the sweaters I had knitted for everyone. I felt good, knowing how surprised they were all going to be. I felt thankful, realizing that I could create such a gift for the people I love. I felt loving, picturing each of them on Christmas morning. I felt loved, anticipating their response to my gift.

I suddenly felt humble. How incredibly, unbelievably

fortunate I am. Because of a birth two thousand years ago, I can know about loving and about giving. Jesus was *given* to us with *love*. That's what it's all about, Christine. Forget the Three Kings and their gifts . . . they had nothing to do with this business of gift-giving at Christmas. Forget about the wrappings; they can never measure up to a manger. Forget all the trimmings, all the price tags, all the gift lists. Forget it all. The bottom line was, and still is, love.

God loves me; God gave me Jesus, a very prized relationship. I love people; I give them gifts. The spirit is the same, but only if I allow it to be.

I started to wrap up all the other gifts, the ones I had purchased in such a panic. In each case, I thanked God for the recipient, and asked that heavenly love flow through this gift. Wow! Something happened. It was a bit like making things for the bazaar. Once I saw them as a channel of God's blessing, like the poodle toilet roll covers, the gifts that seemed so inadequate suddenly became perfect gifts. The wrapping paper, the ribbons, the bow, even the plastic holly were irrelevant, unimportant.

I'm beginning to think that this whole "opting out of today's Christmas" may be more a case of "opting into God's love." Again and again, love becomes the essence of the celebration.

Enough philosophizing. This body needs its rest. At our age, we need all the help we can get!

Good night. God bless.

Pat

17.

JINGLE BELLS
CIRCUIT

When they had seen it, they made known abroad the saying which was told them concerning this child.
—Luke 2:17

December 19

Dear Christine,

Tonight is the annual Christmas party at the office, and I'm sitting here "girding my loins," so to speak. I don't know what it is in the air at this time of the year that incites people to excesses of partymania. I've had invitations to shopping centers, medical centers, drop-in centers, and even waste-disposal centers, all wanting me to come and share the seasonal conviviality with them. I've even had invitations to places I've never heard of. When was the last time you visited the local office of the Society for the Preservation and Public Enjoyment of the Steam Engine Era? They want me to come and share some refreshments with them next Thursday. Ahh . . . what it is to be on the most wanted list for Christmas parties!

But tonight, it's the office party. The whole conglomeration is invited, all three hundred bodies and guests. This multiplies my stress factor three-hundred-fold. For example, do I wear my purple dress (too daring, too bright—what will the boss think?), my brown dress (too dull, too drab—supposing everyone thinks I'm the same?), or my green dress (too young, too short—can't she dress her age?)? Do I arrive exactly on time (doesn't she know about "fashionably late"?) or do

I arrive fashionably late (look at her, trying to make a grand entrance!)? Should I pick daintily at the buffet (what's wrong with our food?) or stick my nose deep in the trough (don't they eat at home?)? Do I dance the mally-wamba (where do you suppose she learned to do that?) or do I stick to the cheek-to-cheek stuff (I hope that's her husband she's with!)?

I know, Chris. It's not as bad as all that. But I feel so vulnerable at these office affairs.

Perhaps it's because I am with a group of people I don't know very well, although I spend most of my waking hours with them. Like most of my co-workers, I obey the dictum that says, "Leave your personal life at home." We all tend to box up our personal lives, keeping them tightly closed, saving any real emotions for outside the office. What we share together are only the petty annoyances and joys of the daily grind: the mail is late, the coffee is cold, the boss is in a good mood.

No wonder I feel such trembling and trepidation when I am faced with a social evening with my co-workers. I don't know them, and they don't know me! What will they think of my party clothes, my conversation, my social graces, even of my husband? Will they like this glimpse of the "real" me? And what will we talk about when the office gossip runs out?

Having put all these thoughts down on paper, they seem so silly and inconsequential, but the feeling of insecurity is real.

The interesting thing is that most of the people who will be there tonight, people I know on a very superficial level, will send (or have sent) a Christmas card wishing me lots of personal joy and happiness. That is part of the paradox of the Chrismas season, I guess.

Enough of this procrastinating, already. I've got to go and get my loins girded.

Pat

Next Day: Good morning. So ask who had a great time at the office party. Me, that's who! How's that for a surprise ending?

"What happened?" you're probably asking.

Remember all those Christmas cards I've been moaning about for these many months? (Ad nauseam, you're probably thinking.) Well, just before we left last night, I read over the letter I started to you. The answer to my dilemma hit me smack in the eye (the working one, that is). I didn't have to send out Christmas cards. I would be seeing half of the people on my list at the party. What better time to give them my own personal greeting, just as I said I wanted to?

I went around to everyone there I knew. I told them how much I appreciated receiving their Christmas cards, and then I said I was delivering my personal card to them. Imagine their surprise when I told them I hoped they'd find some special peace for themselves this season. From there, I talked about my plan to *be* and not to *do*. It was like saying, "Open sesame!" Everyone wanted to talk about my plan. I had real, meaningful conversations with people who I would have bet my last Christmas sticker didn't give a hoot about the spiritual side of Christmas. Which just goes to show I really didn't know them at all.

I'm going to do the same with as many other people as I can find on my list. If I don't run into them somewhere in the next few days, I'll call them.

Do you realize what has happened, Chris? I've finally found a solution to Christmas cards . . . *me* cards! Instead of sending a card, I'm giving people a little bit of me. You can't get much more personal than that.

Suddenly, all these Christmas parties come into perspective. What I've always called the "Jingle Bells Circuit" has a purpose. Perhaps this is why every women's group, men's club, office, school, and factory has a Christmas party. Perhaps we human beings do recognize a need to come together without the daily trappings and just be real people to each other. Perhaps we are all secretly hoping that something special will happen, that some little spark of the Christmas spirit will leap between us.

It gets exciting when you think of all those opportunities to talk to people about Christmas. I don't mean preachy stuff. I mean just talking, one person to another. I mean sharing the good news.

I don't have to worry about what I'm wearing or eating or drinking. I'm just part of the plan. Actually, isn't there a Bible verse that says, "Take no thought for . . . what ye shall eat, or what ye shall drink; nor . . . what ye shall put on"? I'm sure Jesus had something else in mind other than an office Christmas party, but it all boils down to the same thing, doesn't it?
Gotta go. Love and a hug,

Pat

PS. Maybe I will drop in at the office for the Society for the Preservation and Public Enjoyment of the Steam Engine Era and share some refreshments with them. Perhaps I'll share some good news, too.

P.

18.

IN THE
WINK OF AN EYE

Mary kept all these things, and pondered them in her heart.   —Luke 2:19

December 22

Dear Christine,

Have you ever stopped to think "when" it is that it all suddenly happens? "When" is that absolutely perfect moment when you and you alone know it is truly Christmas, and that the Christ child has been born once again in your heart?

On the way home from our writers' group meeting tonight, we started to talk about that "when." We were surprised to find that each of us had a different moment that remained fixed in our mind as the "when" of Christmas. Vickie told us that she vividly remembers the Christmas Eve Communion services, in which the minister always came out onto the front steps of the church to bid people goodnight. As he stood there, it seemed that it always began to snow, and the sight of the snowflakes on his black cloak signalled in Vickie's heart that it was Christmas. The image is simple. Snowflakes on a black cloak.

I asked Cherith if there was a "when" for her. She told me that it was the moment when we put our baby Jesus into the manger in the creche on our mantle. (You probably remember that we always do that just after we get back from church on Christmas Eve.)

My "when" is driving home after the Christmas Eve

service. It's always late at night, of course, and the snowy countryside is shadowed and still. My mind is still full of the sounds of the carols in the church, and my heart is full of the words of the Communion service. Always, somewhere between church and home, "when" happens.

Do you know, Chris, I get tears in my eyes just thinking about those "when" moments. Remember Newfoundland, when you and John were visiting with us, and we drove home from the church at Joe Batt's Arm? There had been a dreadful ice storm, and every possible bush, twig, and blade of grass was covered in ice, and transformed into dazzling sculptures by a thin moon, far out across the ocean. "When" happened just as we came over the hill leading down into the harbor.

In northern Ontario, with the sound of the tires crunching on the frozen roads and the ice crystals hanging in the frigid air, "when" happened.

And here at Stillwater Farm, even on the Christmas Eve that was foggy and warm, "when" happened.

I wonder why it happens. Is it because there is that one moment when our hearts are unreservedly open, when we put aside the cares and worries of this world and go to Bethlehem? Or does "when" happen at the moment when we are suddenly overwhelmed by the love of God shown in the gift of the Son?

Two days left until I expect "when." How wonderful it would be if life were just a series of "when" moments!

Must go. Another small party this evening, and more *me* cards to deliver. Ho, ho, ho!

Pat

December 24: Hi! Didn't get this mailed yet, so I'll just carry on before we go off to church. Actually, it's more of a progress report, because I had a close call this evening. Nearly lost the whole war, and over a minor battle, too. What made it worse was that I had come this far, all the way to Christmas Eve, and aside from a few small slips here and there, I have managed to keep to my resolution and keep my cool in the bargain.

I'm sitting here, trying to calm down before we leave. You see, earlier, Nathan and Cherith wanted to open the Christmas presents tonight. Now, we have always opened our gifts on Christmas Day. However, Gerald let it drop that they always open their gifts on Christmas Eve. It wasn't one of the topics we had discussed before our marriage last year. Suddenly, the song "two different worlds" took on a whole new meaning.

The kids, of course, wanted to do it Gerald's way. I wanted to stick to *our* tradition. They argued and nagged and whined. My temper began to fray. My only argument for sticking to the A.M. schedule was that that's the way we always do it, and I didn't want to change.

What a silly issue to fight over. Does it really matter when the gifts are opened? Yes! But I couldn't say why.

In the end, we compromised. Sort of. I said they could open one gift when we got home from church, and the rest will have to wait until the morning.

For some reason, I have this nagging suspicion that the Christmas Monster is lurking in this somewhere, whispering that it's all going to be ruined if I don't make everyone do it my way. Christmas Day won't be the same, and it will be all my fault for compromising on tradition just to avoid an argument.

Is the glow dimmed? Have I started playing the games of this world's Christmas? I don't think so. Bah, humbug! A pox on this silly argument. I'm off to church. And I'm not going to think about all the gift opening again. If I'm not careful, I'm going to let a foolish disagreement spoil my Christmas Eve. Makes you realize just how fragile our peace is, doesn't it?

Love,

Pat

Later: "Silent night, holy night, All is calm, all is bright." And it is. Calm and bright, that is.

I've just read over what I wrote earlier this evening. What a waste of stewing energy! In the greater scheme of things, opening the Christmas gifts is irrelevant. The only relevancy is the celebration of Christ's birthday.

The "when" happened again tonight. I came to Bethlehem, just as I wanted to. I worshiped with the shepherds and the angels. I basked in the love at the manger.

Afterwards, at home, we opened a gift each, just as the kids wanted to. It didn't make one jot of difference. It was only another extension of the love. After the "when" moment, nothing else is important. Neither traditions nor gifts nor feasts nor revels nor rites.

Silly old me bids you good night.

God bless,

Pat

19.

CHECK THE HALLS, WE'VE LOST THE DOLLY!

Abide in me, and I in you. As the branch cannot bear fruit of itself, except it abide in the vine; no more can ye, except ye abide in me. —John 15:4

December 25

Dear Christine,

Happy Christmas to all of you from all of us!

Well, the great day has almost passed. It's far too late for me to be up, but my little brain is in full gear, and it will take a little while before I get it into sleep mode.

I wonder how many other people feel as overstimulated as I do? There just seems to be too much on Christmas Day to cope with. From opening gifts (in the A.M.!) to driving to church, from enjoying the bountiful feast to searching for a lost dolly, from the moment of waking until this last moment at night, Christmas Day fills our every sense.

There's the overwhelming excitement of the children heading for the tree, the joyous bouyancy of the church service, and the gluttonous anticipation of the bountiful food. Add on the happiness of being with family and friends, the gratitude for a beautiful day, and the enjoyment of the celebration, and you're talking emotional overdrive. (And insomnia!)

Our senses are overwhelmed. Christmas brings all its own sensations: Christmas bells ringing, shouts of glee from children, not to mention junior's new drum, or in our case, Nathan's stereo radio! Our noses are assailed with roasting turkey, steaming plum pudding, candle grease, wood smoke, and pine boughs. Our eyes try to record every moment, from the look on a child's face to the glisten of an icicle outside the window. And our taste buds! It's a wonder they still function after savoring everything from chocolates to macadamia nuts.

See, I told you my brain was in high racing gear! Christmas is almost too much of a good thing. As mother always said when we were overstimulated, "It'll end in tears." And it often does.

Part of me revels in the absolute reality of it all, but part of me is also aware of the thousands who have never experienced Christmas as we do. I feel guilty that we have so much to touch and taste and see and feel.

Are these sensations Christmas, Chris?

No. They can't be. If they were, then there would be no Christmas in parts of the world where the feast was a bowl of rice, and the gifts were nonexistent. There would be no Christmas in the lonely rooms, where loved ones are far away and the table is set for one. Christmas could never come to the hospital bedside, to the jail cell, or to the psychiatric ward.

What I have experienced today is not the Christmas of the heart. It is wonderful, but if it were all taken away from me tomorrow, I would still have Christmas.

Today has been a glorious birthday party. But, even with no party, there is still a birthday. The true party is safe and secure in my heart. Happy birthday, Jesus!

Love and the biggest Christmas hug I can find.

Good night all (at last),

Pat

20.

THE
PARTY'S OVER . . .

*The God of hope fill you with all joy and peace in believ-
ing, that ye may abound in hope.* —Romans 15:13

December 26

Dear Christine,

Anticlimax hangs in the air like a dark pall. My head aches, my stomach hurts, and I'm scratchy-eyed and crabby. I'm not alone, either. Splodgy just cuffed Tabby. No doubt he is also suffering from a surfeit of Christmas.

I don't feel like cleaning up the debris in the living room; I don't want to start doing something clever with the leftover turkey; I don't care if I never hear another carol as long as I live. So there!

Is there anything in the world worse than the day after any event you've waited for and longed for and dreamed of? No wonder women suffer from postpartum depression. Do you suppose that is my problem today? Do you suppose the whole world is suffering from postpartum depression? The babe is born; the suspense is over. Life must go on, and living must return to normal.

In the ordinary physical sense, this is true. However, I don't believe it's supposed to be true in the spiritual sense. When you think of it, Chris, all Christians should be feeling a wonderful sense of excitement, of anticipation. The Babe is born, and yes, life must go on, but living will never again return to what it was.

Living takes on a whole new dimension. The hopelessness is gone. The feeling that nothing is worthwhile, that there is no purpose to our lives, no hope for our afterlives . . . that has all been changed irrevocably by the birth of this Babe.

Wow! This kind of thinking certainly puts my messy living room and turkey leftovers into perspective! Enough of this "morning after the night before" depression. I'm going to make everyone put on the sweaters I knitted (which, by the way, were a 101 percent success, due no doubt to the fact that no one was suffering from the guilts because Martyr Mom "had" to knit them a sweater), and I'm going to take the whole gang out skiing in the back forty. That should blow away the bad tempers. Wonder if I can persuade Splodgy to come along in a back pack?

See you later,

Pat

Much, Much later: We must stop having these midnight trysts, Chris. It's hard on my required eight hours. (Actually, as one of my birthday cards once said, "If I'd known I was going to live this long, I would have taken better care of myself." I'm just trying to make up for past neglect.)

Christmas Day is well and truly over . . . in fact, according to my clock we're into post-Boxing Day right now. The celebration may be over, but the song lives on.

I honestly feel as if today, and every day since the birth in Bethlehem, is "the first day of the rest of my life." (I sure am full of quotes tonight . . . must be something about the air after midnight.)

Do you realize that we Christians can have Christmas every day? No, not that frazzling, running, rushing, doing, doing, doing Christmas that I was so determined to avoid, but the Christmas that keeps the glow in our hearts, the sure knowledge that we have been given a gift beyond any worldly measure.

Wow! I'd better stop. I'm getting my brain all revved up again.

Christmas every day. Sounds great to me. Happy Christmas, again. And again.

Love and another Christmassy hug,

Pat

PS. Going skiing was a good idea. We all came home rejuvenated and ready for the deviled turkey legs. Except for Splodgy.

PPS. The sweaters fit beautifully. Which goes to show what you can do when you're not trying.

PPPS. Do you suppose there would ever be a market for a good cookbook called, *A Thousand and One Things to Do with Leftover Turkey so that No One in Your Family Would Ever Suspect It Was the Same Bird You Had for Christmas*? I think so to. Shall we consider it as a joint project? We could call it something like, *Turkey Lurkey's Last Stand*. OK, OK. I'll go to bed quietly. Nighty-night.

P.

21.

SOUNDING BRASS
AND TINKLING CYMBALS

Though I speak with the tongues of men and of angels, and have not charity, I am become as sounding brass, or a tinkling cymbal.　　　　　—I Corinthians 13:1

January 3

Dear Christine,

Happy New Year! Here we are again, sitting at the beginning of a bright, shiny new year. Last year at this time, I was whining and moaning about Christmas. This year? Well, this year, I feel just fine, thank you. Perhaps even a little smug.

I feel like you and I have been on a long journey together, exploring unknown terrain, looking for the Lost Treasure of Christmas.

I wish I'd kept copies of all those letters I wrote to you last year. I have this nagging suspicion that there is a common thread in each one. If I could read them again, I'm sure I'd find clues that would lead me to the treasure I seek. I've been thinking about those clues today, sitting here in my quiet house, savoring the delights of postseason peace. I have a feeling that the treasure I've been looking for is right under my nose.

When I think back on all those occasions when I wrote to you about my quest for the real Christmas, I'm pretty sure that I always ended up at the same place. That place? Love.

Love. Simple, so simple, and yet, all this time, I've been missing it. Love is the Lost Treasure of Christmas.

When I fussed over how to send out Christmas cards,

didn't it finally boil down to a message of love to the world around me?

When I made a martyr of myself knitting sweaters on the beach, didn't I finally realize that without love as the motive, there was no point in knitting them?

Didn't I learn from Audrey that love is the force behind every item we make for the Christmas bazaars—and not the money we'll earn from them?

And didn't I decide that it was God's love for us that gave us the seasons so that we could prepare ourselves for the coming of the Son?

Remember my "attitude of gratitude"? That came from love, too, and a thankfulness for that love.

The Santa Claus parade. Was love there? It was when I remember the small group walking behind the sleigh.

And the Christmas Monster. He was the antipathy of love. He showed me that Christmas comes out of love, not out of guilt.

Love was the reason I agreed to direct the Sunday school concert.

Love is the reason I carry on traditions. Without them, there'd be no occasion to reflect on that love.

I learned to fight the battle of the kitchen with love. I also learned it's OK to let someone else do the fighting for me.

When my Christmas tree attacked me, I learned to love it, not for what it is, but for what it symbolized—the living presence in Christmas.

When we all came together at the Sunday school concert, there was a bond of love between us.

Gift shopping became so much easier when I thought

of the gifts as vehicles of not just my love, but God's love as well.

And remember how excited I was when I discovered that the Jingle Bells Circuit could be part of a loving plan to spread the good news?

In that special "when" moment on Christmas Eve, it is love that makes Christmas happen again.

On Christmas Day, even without a glorious birthday party, love would still celebrate Christmas in our hearts.

And when it's all over, love remains, constant, bright . . . daily leading us, daily filling us.

Chris, the treasure I have been seeking is God's love. And all the fuss and bother and worry and confusion . . . the anxiety, the pain, the tension, and the guilt . . . the rushing, the hurrying, the doing . . . all of the trappings of the season, the unrealities and the self-ishness, all of these are just sounding brass and tinkling cymbals. For, "if I have not love . . ." Well, if I don't have love, all I do have is the Christmas of this world. And I've opted out of that . . . forever.

I've opted into God's love.

Thanks, Christine, for listening to me moan and groan, agonize and apologize for the past year. Every-one needs a friendly shoulder now and then. Thanks for being mine.

Love, love, and a hug,

Pat

ABOUT THE AUTHOR

Patricia Wilson lives on a rural Ontario farm with her husband and children. She has had a wide variety of jobs and occupations and is currently the Manager of Marketing and Communications for the St. Lawrence Parks Commission of the Ontario government.

Ms. Wilson stays involved in a number of community activities, such as theater, the community library, and choirs. She has also written *Have You Met My Divine Uncle George?*, *Who Put All These Cucumbers in My Garden?*, and *The Daisies Are Still Free.*